To:

_____

From:

_____

DEAR DAD...

Selected by
Shifra Stein

THE C. R. GIBSON COMPANY · NORWALK, CONNECTICUT

# DEAR DAD...

## THE MAN WE CALL DAD

For the man who gave me life, I thank you, Lord. For the wonderful man we call Dad.

For his joking, his eternal optimism, the joy he sheds, the friends he's always made.

For the home he provided for us. For the courage and determination with which he bucked the world for his family.

Dear Lord, for this father I thank you. For this wonderful dad.

I thank you for the lessons he taught us:

To be honest—never to take so much as a postage stamp.

To be brave—that so long as you did right you had nothing to fear.

To believe in yourself, because you're often the only one who will.

To be grateful, to appreciate little things. A bucket of cold water from the well, a tart red apple, a bird on a telephone wire.

For these lessons, dear Lord, I thank you.

I am glad that of all the men you might have chosen, it was he who brought me into being. Thank you for this father, Lord.

Thank you for this man we call Dad!

Marjorie Holmes

## WHAT I WANT

I don't want a pipe and I don't want a watch,
I don't want cigars or a bottle of Scotch.
I don't want a thing your money can buy,
I don't want a shirt or a four-in-hand tie.
If you really would make this old heart of mine glad,
I just want to know you're still fond of your dad.

You women folk say, and believe it I can,
"It's so terribly hard to buy things for a man!"
And from all that I've heard I am sure it must be.
Well, I don't want you spending your money on me,
The joy that I crave in a store can't be had.
I just want to know you're still fond of your dad.

Get on with your shopping; give others the stuff!
For me just a hug and a kiss are enough!
Just come in at Christmas with love in your eye
And tell me you think I'm a Pretty Swell guy.
With that for my gift I can never be sad.
I just want to know you're still fond of your dad.

EDGAR A. GUEST

## DADDY WON'T LISTEN TO REASON

I used to feel that children were little empty vessels
to be filled with pure reason. But events of my later,
or paternal, years have taught me what a precarious
hold we have on logic, and how sometimes we find
ourselves hanging onto words by our fingernails, like
an early movie hero hanging onto a boxcar, while
beneath us is a vast pit of human misunderstanding.

After a few minutes' talk with my youngest
daughter I sometimes sit staring at the wallpaper and
reflecting that if my dear old professor of logic tried
that "Man is immortal: Socrates is a man" routine
on my Mary, in no time at all she would have him
admitting that Socrates was running somewhere,
and trying to prove that tigers wouldn't like the way
he tasted, if tigers weren't birds.

I'll say to her, for instance, when my wife has left
me to mind her for a while, "Now look, I'm just
going around the corner for some cigarettes. I don't
want you to leave this house till I get back. I'll only
be gone a minute. Do you understand?"

"Yes, Daddy." This very innocently, as she gets
ready to break me down.

I eye her suspiciously and add, "No matter what
happens, or which one of your friends comes
around and asks you to come and play.
Understand?"

"Yes, Daddy."

I start off, feeling the way I do when I'm passing a
little boy with a water gun. I think, with gestures,
"That's clear enough. Leave the house . . . no matter

which friends . . . "

"Daddy."

I duck my head.

"No matter *who* tells me to leave the house?"

I whip around. "Nobody's going to tell you to leave the house. You just see that you stay here."

"I know nobody will tell me to leave the house," Mary says.

"Fine." I start off.

"But if somebody does tell me to leave the house, I'm not to leave, am I?"

"NO!" I say, wishing she'd stop playing with me like a cat with a mouse.

"Not even if a policeman came along and said I had to leave the house?" Mary asks.

"What would a policeman be doing coming around and telling you to leave the house?" I yelp. "Policemen are all busy—being policemen."

"Yes," Mary agrees with a sweet smile and a sigh.

I start off again.

"Do I have to leave if Grandma comes along and says, 'You leave this house, Mary'?"

"No—yes—OKAY! If Mummy, Grandma or a policeman tell you to leave—BUT THASS ALL! Why you gotta drag your grandmother into it?" (You'll notice that here, along with not being very logical, I'm not even speaking English any more.)

"And if a fireman came along and told me that the house is on fire, I'd have to leave, wouldn't I? Or if a lot of soldiers told me to leave, or a skunk got in, or my Sunday-school teacher told me to leave, or if I looked out the window and saw a lion coming in the front door, should I leave then, Daddy?"

My kids can take little bricks of pure logic and make reasonable constructions out of them that I know are stuck together with bubble gum and puffed wheat but I can't prove anything . . . .

All in all, there's something about a child's logic that can't be equated to the adult mind. It's the same with those, What-do-they-do? questions. I've been trying to figure out for years what my youngest means when she asks what flowers do. A flower sits. Or sort of sticks. A flower is. Flowers stick around. A wheel rounds. Giraffes go around with a long neck. One time Mary asked me what makes a knock in a motor. I said, well, it might be a main bearing or it might be a connecting rod. She said, if there was a knock in your motor, which would it be?

I still wonder what the answer is sometimes as I go up to bed, dragging the shredded evening paper after me.

ROBERT THOMAS ALLEN

*In her book, "How It Was," Mary Welch Hemingway recalls her father as a man who guided her in the direction of individualism:*

He was a man of instant blooming temper, but his patience, answering my questions to help me understand the ferocious world of grownups, daily nourished my devotion to him. I learned what made the bogs grow, why birds chose one nesting site instead of another. When I was perplexed by Chapter 34 of Exodus, the Lord "forgiving iniquity . . . (but) visiting the iniquity of the fathers upon the children," my father explained the history of the Bible and the fanaticism of its early compilers.

One evening as we were splashing softly through the twilight, he pointed out the chair-shaped formation of stars emerging from the blue of the northern sky. "That constellation is Cassiopeia. It is about as far to the right of the North Star, see, as the pointers of the Dipper are to the left. Now, Dearidoo, if you were up there sitting on the North Star looking at Cassiopeia, it would look like an *M* to you. *M*, for Mary. And if you could see it from a million miles to the northeast of us, it would look like a *W* to you. So your initials are written in the stars." I remembered Cassiopeia, and did not question his astronomy.

Of the knowledge and thought my father poured over me those summers, one gift came as we were walking toward the big white boat across a pasture full of sheep. We watched them run witlessly ahead, aside and astern of us, and I thought them hilarious, squeezed my father's hand and said, "Aren't they silly, Papa? They could hurt themselves running so blindly."

My father laughed and as we escaped the milling animals said, "Remember this, Mary. Never be a sheep. Never follow a leader only because he is ahead of you. Take time to look around and see for yourself if you are going in the right direction." I must have been eight or nine years old that morning.

The words that a father speaks to his children in the privacy of home are not heard by the world, but, as in whispering-galleries, they are clearly heard at the end and by posterity.

JEAN PAUL RICHTER

*Reese Sarda joined the growing number of young fathers who elect to spend a few years "mothering. Here he remembers a not-so-hypothetical 15-minute segment of a typical day with his two daughters.*

It is afternoon. There is bread baking in the oven. It will be done in five minutes. Suddenly Inga wakes up and begins crying. She's a half hour early. Sigrid is sitting peacefully by the toy box, puttering with something.

Should I take out the bread early and hope it won't be soggy inside? Or should I leave it in the oven and go up and change Inga and bring her down and hope the bread won't dry out? Or should I get her bottle ready and let her wait the five minutes that it takes? The last is the most practical. As long as she's crying, "Hey, I'm hungry!" I know she is safe and sound.

The baby is crying lightly, the bread is baking and the bottle of formula is being heated. I open the oven, take out one loaf, turn it out of the pan and thump it. A nice, resonant sound—the bread is finished. I've just reached in for the second loaf when out of the corner of my eye I see Sigrid dashing across the room, shoelaces flapping dangerously. That's why she's been so quiet! She's been fastidiously working on the bows I'd tied 30 minutes before.

Sigrid is going too fast for comfort. I put the second loaf of bread, still in the pan, on the counter and rush into the living room and grab Sigrid before she trips. While I'm tying her left shoe in a more challenging combination of bows, the water in which the formula is heating suddenly boils over the saucepan.

At that instant the baby stops crying, arousing my suspicions—and the telephone rings, arousing exasperation. I finish with Sigrid's left shoelace and rush to get to the stove before the boiling water puts out the gas flame. Then I pick up the phone.

Sigrid glares at me. She is furious. First I've undone the beautiful job she'd done of untying her left shoe and now I am completely ignoring her untied right shoe, thus saddling her with a terrible case of lopsidedness. She starts sobbing as if the world's greatest tragedy had just occurred.

"Hold on a minute," I say into the telephone—it's my favorite telephone phrase—and I dash upstairs to see why Inga has stopped crying. She's asleep. By the time I get back, Sigrid has forgotten about her shoe and is using the phone receiver and cord as a yo-yo, whacking the receiver on the floor. I get the phone back, which means more tears from Sigrid.

Lynn, who is usually very thoughtful about not disturbing me at my work (unlike the majority of providing mates), is on the phone. She has called for no other reason than to be friendly.

"What's going on there?" she asks.

I sense an accusatory tone and snap, "Everything's fine."

At that moment Sigrid notices the bread pan and tries to reach it. I call, "No, no! It's hot!" She pauses in her efforts. A teasing grin crosses her face. I can hear the wheels turning as she wonders: Does Daddy mean it?

There are some lessons you let your child learn through experience after she's failed to heed a warning, but burning her hand isn't one of them. "Hold on a minute," I tell Lynn, and then carry Sigrid out of the kitchen. She's crying again. I return to the kitchen, push the bread well out of reach and win the race with Sigrid back to the yo-yo. She storms off. Everything she wants to do today I mess up.

Before I get the phone to my ear Inga begins crying again. An alarm goes off inside me. This time it's not because she's hungry or wet. It is something else—something that can't be put off. "I'll call you later," I tell Lynn, and race upstairs. One of Inga's legs is caught between the crib bars. I free her and pick her up, comfort her and change her diaper. All the while I listen carefully to Sigrid's progress on the stairs. As long as she's going up, she's fine. She reaches the top just as we are ready to go down. With Inga over my shoulder and Sigrid under my arm, we head for the living room. A moment later I'm sitting down, holding the baby's bottle in one hand and struggling to untie a knot in Sigrid's right shoelace with the other.

The scene took about 15 minutes. It could hardly be called a crisis—it was just one series of nonscheduled involvements that fill the parenting schedule daily. I was mentally alert every minute; yet what was I thinking about? I don't know what I was thinking about.

FIRST LESSON
The thing to remember about fathers is, they're
    men.
A girl has to keep it in mind.
They are dragon-seekers, bent on improbable
    rescues.
Scratch any father, you find
Someone chock-full of qualms and romantic terrors,
Believing change is a threat—
Like your first shoes with heels on, like your first
    bicycle
It took such months to get.

Walk in strange woods, they warn you about the
    snakes there.
Climb, and they fear you'll fall.
Books, angular boys, or swimming in deep water—
Fathers mistrust them all.
Men are the worriers. It is difficult for them
To learn what they must learn:
How you have a journey to take and very likely,
For a while, will not return.

PHYLLIS McGINLEY

## DISCOVERY OF A FATHER

One of the strangest relationships in the world is that between father and son. I know it now from having sons of my own.

A boy wants something very special from his father. You hear it said that fathers want their sons to be what they feel they cannot themselves be, but I tell you it also works the other way. I know that as a small boy I wanted my father to be a certain thing he was not. I wanted him to be a proud, silent, dignified father. When I was with other boys and he passed along the street, I wanted to feel a flow of pride: 'There he is. That is my father.'

But he wasn't such a one. He couldn't be. It seemed to me then that he was always showing off. Let's say someone in our town had got up a show. They were always doing it. The druggist would be in it, the shoe-store clerk, the horse-doctor, and a lot of women and girls. My father would manage to get the chief comedy part. It was, let's say, a Civil War play and he was a comic Irish soldier. He had to do the most absurd things. They thought he was funny, but I didn't.

I thought he was terrible. I didn't see how Mother could stand it. She even laughed with the others. Maybe I would have laughed if it hadn't been my father.

Often I was filled with bitterness, and sometimes I wished he wasn't my father. I'd even invent another man as my father. To protect my mother I'd make up stories of a secret marriage that for some strange reason never got known. As though some man, say, the president of a railroad company or maybe a Congressman, had married my mother, thinking his wife was dead and then it turned out she wasn't.

Now they had to hush it up, but I got born just the same. I wasn't really the son of my father. Somewhere in the world there was a very dignified, quite wonderful man who was really my father. I even made myself half-believe these fancies.

And then there came a certain night. Mother was away from home. Maybe there was a church that night. Father came in. He'd been off somewhere for two or three weeks. He found me alone in the house, reading by the kitchen table.

It had been raining and he was very wet. He sat and looked at me for a long time, not saying a word. I was startled, for there was on his face the saddest look I had ever seen. He sat for a time, his clothes dripping. Then he got up.

'Come on with me,' he said.

I got up and went with him out of the house. I was filled with wonder, but I wasn't afraid. We went along a dirt road that led down into a valley, about a mile out of town, where there was a pond. We walked in silence. The man who was always talking had stopped his talking.

I didn't know what was up and had the queer feeling that I was with a stranger. I don't know whether my father intended it so. I don't think he did.

The pond was quite large. It was still raining hard

and there were flashes of lightning followed by thunder. We were on a grassy bank at the pond's edge when my father spoke, and in the darkness and rain his voice sounded strange.

'Take off your clothes,' he said. Still filled with wonder, I began to undress. There was a flash of lightning and I saw that he was already naked.

Naked, we went into the pond. Taking my hand he pulled me in. It may be that I was too frightened, too full of a feeling of strangeness, to speak. Before that night my father had never seemed to pay any attention to me.

'And what is he up to now?' I kept asking myself. I did not swim very well, but he put my hand on his shoulder and struck out into the darkness.

He was a man with big shoulders, a powerful swimmer. In the darkness I could feel the movement of his muscles. We swam to the far edge of the pond and then back to where we had left our clothes. The rain continued and the wind blew. Sometimes my father swam on his back and when he did, he took my hand in his large powerful one and moved it over so that it rested always on his shoulder. Sometimes there would be a flash of lightning and I could see his face quite clearly.

It was as it was earlier, in the kitchen, a face filled with sadness. There would be the momentary glimpse of his face and then again the darkness, the wind and the rain. In me there was a feeling I had never known before.

It was a feeling of closeness. It was something

strange. It was as though there were only we two in the world. It was as though I had been jerked suddenly out of myself, out of my world of the schoolboy, out of a world in which I was ashamed of my father.

He had become blood of my blood; the strong swimmer and I the boy clinging to him in the darkness. We swam in silence and in silence we dressed in our wet clothes, and went home.

There was a lamp lighted in the kitchen, and when we came in, the water dripping from us, there was my mother. She smiled at us. I remember that she called us 'boys.' 'What have you boys been up to?' she asked, but my father did not answer. As he had begun the evening's experience with me in silence, so he ended it. He turned and looked at me. Then he went, I thought, with a new and strange dignity, out of the room.

I climbed the stairs to my own room, undressed in darkness and got into bed. I couldn't sleep and did not want to sleep. For the first time I knew that I was the son of my father. He was a storyteller as I was to be. It may be that I even laughed a little softly there in the darkness. If I did, I laughed knowing that I would never again be wanting another father.

SHERWOOD ANDERSON

*Art Linkletter's book, "Oops!" is a funny collection of surprises from "the mouths of babes." Here are a few samples of what children had to say about their dads:*

One young man flatly told me that his dad had clearly instructed him not to tell what he did.

"Why not?" I urged.

"Because it's a kind of a funny word."

"Well, suppose you just try it out on me and see if I think it's funny?"

"All right," he said hesitantly. "He's a stupidvisor."

---

"What do you want to be?"

"A fireman."

"Why pick that?"

"Because my dad says I'm dumb enough to be one."

"What does your dad do?"

"He's a fireman."

---

"What makes your mother the maddest?"

"When my dad comes home, takes off his shoes, opens a bottle of beer, sits down in front of the TV set, and whistles at all the pretty girls on the program."

---

"What's the funniest thing you've seen this summer?"

"Dad came home, hit Mom on the back of her lap with a chair, and she threw a cherry pie at him."

The seven-year-old child of a famous movie star unconsciously revealed the conditioning his surroundings had worked on his philosophy of life. He had told me that he wanted to be an actor in motion pictures and when I asked him why, a blissful expression spread across his face. "I'd like the life," he confided.

"What would that be like?" I asked him cautiously.

"Well," he said, "a movie star wakes up at ten and has breakfast in bed. Then he takes a limousine to the studio and kisses girls all day. Then he has dinner in some nightclub, and if he wants to, he marries the prettiest girl late that night."

I didn't try to disillusion him. But I had a lot of fun with his father the next day on the phone.

---

"What can your dad do around the house?"
"Well, once he tried to fix the car."
"What happened?"
"We had to get a new car."

---

"What does your dad do for fun?"
"He chases cats."
"What does your mother do for fun?"
"She puts ice cubes in my father's beer while he's out chasing cats."

---

"Who's the boss in your house?"
"My mother. Because she's the one who tells Daddy where he can go!"

from THE PEOPLE, YES
A father sees a son nearing manhood.
What shall he tell that son?
"Life is hard; be steel; be a rock."
And this might stand him for the storms
and serve him for humdrum and monotony
and guide him amid sudden betrayals
and tighten him for slack moments.
"Life is a soft loam; be gentle; go easy."
And this too might serve him.
Brutes have been gentled where lashes failed.
The growth of a frail flower in a path up
has sometimes shattered and split a rock.
A tough will counts. So does desire.
So does a rich soft wanting.
Without rich wanting nothing arrives.
Tell him too much money has killed men
and left them dead years before burial:
the quest of lucre beyond a few easy needs
has twisted good enough men
sometimes into dry thwarted worms.
Tell him time as a stuff can be wasted.
Tell him to be a fool every so often
and to have no shame over having been a fool
yet learning something out of every folly
hoping to repeat none of the cheap follies
thus arriving at intimate understanding
of a world numbering many fools.
Tell him to be alone often and get at himself
and above all tell himself no lies about himself
whatever the white lies and protective fronts

he may use amongst other people.
Tell him solitude is creative if he is strong
and the final decisions are made in silent rooms.
Tell him to be different from other people
if it comes natural and easy being different.
Let him have lazy days seeking his deeper motives.
Let him seek deep for where he is a born natural.
   Then he may understand Shakespeare
   and the Wright brothers, Pasteur, Pavlov,
   Michael Faraday and free imaginations
bringing changes into a world resenting change.
   He will be lonely enough
   to have time for the work
   he knows as his own.

CARL SANDBURG

## MY FATHER

My father is short, honest, dark, and very handsome. He's good, he's a good man. He was born in Mexico, and brought up in Brooklyn. My father worked hard in school. He loved God and the church and his parents. At one time in his life he was going to be a minister, but he became a scientist instead. He has a vision of how science can play the major role in saving the world. This vision puts a light into his eyes.

While he was with UNESCO . . . . he was trying to finish a book, which took him eight years to write. A basic text in physics. I seriously thought he would not ever complete that book, that it was like an eternally incomplete project he had to have to keep himself worn out. And I thought he was afraid to get it printed. But it was published while he was still in Paris. It's beautiful. The introduction is preceded by a picture of a huge rock suspended over the ocean. The picture makes you want to sit down heavily on the floor, or throw a paperweight out the window and watch it hit the sidewalk. There are little bits of human philosophy preceding each chapter, over eight hundred pictures, and the book is dedicated to "my wife, Joan, and my three daughters, Pauline, Joanie, and Mimi." And on page 274 there is a drawing which illustrates how an image is projected onto a television screen, and the image being projected is of a familiar-looking girl with long black hair, who stands holding a guitar.

In my estimation, my old man got his sense of

humor back when he left Paris, and returned to the States. Toward the end of a course he was teaching at Harvard, a crash summer course, based on his book, he gave what he later described to me as the "demonstration of the century." He told the class that he was going to give an example of jet propulsion. He had a little red wagon brought in, and then he took the fire extinguisher off the wall and sat down in the wagon and jet propelled himself in circles around the front of the room, explaining, at the top of his voice, exactly what was happening technically. The students stood on their chairs and gave him an ovation, and it was all so overwhelming that he repeated the experiment. He shouted halfway through it for someone to open the door, and shot himself out into the hall, and disappeared. When he came back the bell had rung and the class was still there, cheering.

My mother planted my father and herself in a beautiful place in Carmel Valley, about one mile from my house, and not far from Pauline. A while after they began to be settled, I asked him if he could give himself permission to enjoy the luxury of his new home, his swimming pool, the endless beauty of the hills around. He tried to avoid my question by making a joke, but I said I was serious. We were sitting on the floor on a nice carpet, and he smoothed his hands over it as he leaned back against the wall. He looked very brown and Mexican in that moment, and I watched his profile against the valley hills as he struggled with himself. He said something about other people in the world, and about hunger. Then he looked up and gave me a smile of such a combination of things. "Yes, honey," he said, "I think I can enjoy it . . if I keep myself busy enough . . ."

A WONDERFUL MAN
My father carries a pearl-handled knife
With three steel blades that are big as life.
One is longest, and one is littler,
And the shortest one is the sharpest whittler.

My father whittles out whistles from sticks,
And he uses his knife when there're things to fix,
And he whittles me darts and arrows and bows
And boats, and other such things as those.

And sometimes he says, "Would you like to use
My knife to whittle whatever you choose?"
So I whittle something as well as I can—
Say, but my father's a wonderful man!

AILEEN FISHER

*With loving nostalgia, writer Janet Gillespie
introduces us to her father in "A Joyful Noise."
Here, "Pop" is both wise and touching as he
attempts to prepare his child for life outside the
home.*

We loved surprises in our family, and during the
period of preparation we built up tension about the
surprise in various ways. As the moment of truth
drew near we worked the victim into a frenzy of
anticipation, and when the surprise finally broke we
expected a violent reaction. It wouldn't be too much
to say that we would have been gratified if the
person had fallen to the ground insensible or had
had some sort of mild seizure from surprise.

I removed my napkin from the pile on my chair
and began the ceremonies, while everybody stood
around to watch my reactions and tell me all the
circumstances leading up to the purchase of the
present.

"Mine cost fifty cents," said Bobs proudly.

Pop never had the faintest idea what was in the
packages Mum had bought and given in their
names, but he always said he had spent much time
and thought selecting them.

"I hope you realize the trouble I went to to get
just that color," he said.

"Oh, I do," I said. "How did you ever guess? It's
just what I wanted."

After breakfast Pop and I went out to look at the
day and decide what kind of expedition would be
suitable with the wind and tide provided by God.

Pop, who never let a milestone go by without a bit of homely philosophy, now said I had reached a new stage in my life. Pretty soon, he said, I would be a woman and he knew I would be a joy in the home. Here he broke down momentarily, but got a fresh grip on himself and went on.

"I know you want what every nice girl wants."

"What's that?" I asked, while he struggled for control.

"A happy home like ours, a good chap for a husband—better than your old man," he put in humbly.

"I do not," I said. "You're the best father in the world."

"Far from it," said Pop, "as your mother will tell you. However, now that you're growing older you'll realize that you have a pretty face and the fellows will be around. You may think they want a fast, hard girl, but, no, they want a friend, a sister."

He then croaked out the first line of a ghastly song called "I want a girl just like the girl that married dear old Dad."

"For Pete's sake, Pop," I said.

"Well, it's true," he quavered.

I saw it was time to put a stop to the revolting drivel.

"Now that I'm grown up," I said, "how about letting me cut my hair like everybody else? It's bad enough," I said bitterly, "that Baba makes me wear long stockings when everybody in my class wears socks."

"What's all this about hair and socks?" asked Pop, abruptly abandoning his dear-old-Dad role.

"Well, how would you like to have everybody say you looked like Alice in Wonderland?" I asked.

"The chances of that are very slight," said Pop, running his hand over his bald spot.

However, he was now bored with the whole subject and said it looked like a good breeze and what about a sailing picnic? I said that would be perfect and could we have chops?

"Not only could we have chops," said Pop, now completely restored to his normal merry self. "You see before you a tinted photograph of the man who will cook them for you."

## A FATHER SPEAKS OF FATHERS

I suppose that Father's Day is a good idea, though there seems something pretty pointed in the fact that no one thought of putting a red mark on the calendar for the Old Man until long after there had been a Mother's Day, an Arbor Day, a Labor Day, and a Ground Hog Day. Since I am a father myself it might appear immodest were I to suggest that fathers are often found superior to ground hogs—or, at least, more useful around the first of the month than ground hogs. However, such a suggestion might be taken as an indication that fathers are ungrateful for their blessings and this might, in turn, start a movement to abolish Father's Day until we learn humility.

For my part, however, I confess myself interested in fatherhood and I simply do not go along with those who contend that about the only time a father is worth having about is in the Spring when it is time to fertilize the flower beds. It has been my privilege to know a great many fathers and I have found them to be charming creatures. True, many of them are shy, particularly those that have large, noisy families, but they respond marvelously to kindness, and I am not exaggerating when I say that the average father will, if treated with tolerance and respect, become a fine companion and pet and may be readily trained to retrieve balls, short sticks, and other small objects.

There are many things to bear in mind in the raising of a good, reliable father. It is well to remember that many of them are proud, sensitive animals, that they bruise easily, and that they thrive on peace and quiet.

Feeding is recognized by some of the most successful father fanciers as a problem deserving special attention. All too often the selection of his diet is left to the mother who, in most cases, insists on feeding father the sort of things which she prefers, which is to say, table scraps. A father can subsist just so long on salads, creamed side dishes, canned vegetables, gelatin desserts, and sandwiches with the crust cut off them. Then, unless something is done, he begins to sneak off at meal time. This is often confused with infidelity. Just remember that more marital discord is created by the absence of steak and French fries than by the presence of blondes and redheads.

Another common fault in the rearing of fathers is the tendency to educate them more than they want to be educated. It is a mistake to try to elevate a father's tastes because fathers are interested in creature comforts and, hence, do not like sopranos. A father, for instance, thinks of chairs only in terms of leaning back, and does not respond kindly to the information that he may, in the future, sit gingerly on the edge of an antique. He will doggedly refuse to believe that the antique is attractive and there is no use trying to educate him to any other point of view.

Similarly, efforts to teach fathers to discriminate between guest towels and the everyday variety usually fail. In fine, the sooner it is recognized that a father would rather be comfortable than socially acceptable, the quicker you will develop an animal which, while often disheveled and embarrassing in the presence of company, is a reliable creature to send downstairs late at night when it is believed that a burglar is at the Community Plate.

There is so much to be said on this topic that one is tempted to go on forever. I notice that it is almost dark, however, and I have been instructed to sprinkle the grass as soon as the sun is down, so I will have to quit. Incidentally, if you are really interested in producing a better father, sprinkle the darned grass yourself sometime. I'm not the only person in this family who can nurse a nozzle.

The point of all this is really quite simple. Just bear in mind, particularly around Father's Day, that the more fathers are treated like people the more they act like people. Whether this is worth all the trouble that is involved is something for you to decide.

RALF KIRCHER

FIRST BOOKS

The importance of exercising extreme care in choosing the books which your child will read and reread cannot be overemphasized. Lack of intelligent discrimination in this matter can discourage a child to such a degree that he may never come to know the wonderful World of Books. Here are some questions to ask yourself about any book you are considering for your child:

1. If he hits you with it, will it hurt?

2. What will be the effect on the book if the child takes it into the bath with him and gives it a good scrubbing with Daddy's toothbrush? Finally (and of least importance), what will be the effect on Daddy?

3. If half the pages are ripped out and torn to shreds, will it affect the story line?

4. In the event that the child demands it be read over and over again for as much as an hour, will it produce nausea?

5. Is the volume small enough to be quickly and easily hidden in the event that you *have* been forced to read it over and over again for as much as an hour and it *has* produced nausea?

6. Is the type bold enough to be read through a thin layer of strained squash?

7. Will it fill a specific need? Is it exciting enough to distract him while you spoon him full of cereal, or is it sufficiently soporific to lull him to sleep after a wild day at the sandbox?

If the answers to these questions seem to be in the book's favor and the cost isn't much more than four or five dollars, it won't do much harm to buy it.

Once you've bought the book, catchily entitled *Cocky-Locky Bakes Some Cookie-Lookies,* and taken it home, what then? Should you just hand it to him and say, "Here's a quarter book I brung ya"? Definitely not! Hold on to it. It's money in the bank. Keep it under wraps until, in the normal course of events, a crisis arises. Then say, in your most casual manner, "If you don't stop eating the leaves off Mommy's nice philodendron, I won't give you the pretty new book I bought you." If you manage just the proper tone, he'll stop. He might even spit out what he has in his mouth. You then have him—and philodendron pulp—in the palm of your hand.

He sits down beside you on the sofa, and you begin to read. *"One bright sunshiny day, Cocky-Locky got up and said, 'Isn't this a bright sunshiny day! I think I'll bake some cookie-lookies!' "* As you struggle through to the end of the tale, your docile little lamb leaps from the sofa and heads for his playroom. He's back in a flash with a tall stack of all the books he's ever owned. He nestles down beside you, his face lit with a happy, anticipatory smile. There's nothing for it but to take the top book off the pile and begin to read: *"One bright sunshiny day, Bunny-No-Good was hopping down the path. As he hopped, he passed seven naughty dandelions. 'Naughty Dandelions,' he said. . . ."*

Later—much later—you go numb and it isn't so bad.

STANLEY AND JANICE BERENSTAIN

## HOLDING THE BABY

Biology has been unscrupulous enough to distinguish markedly against women, and men have seized upon this advantage to press the belief that, since the bearing of children is exclusively the province of women, it must be that the caring for them belongs properly to the same sex. Yet how ridiculous this is. Most things which have to be done for children should tax the intelligence of no one. Men profess lack of ability to wash baby's face simply because they believe there's no great fun in the business, at either end of the sponge. Man even pretends that he doesn't know how to hold the baby. From this has grown the shockingly transparent fallacy that holding a baby correctly is one of the fine arts; or, perhaps, a wonderful intuition which has come down after centuries of effort to women only.

"The thing that surprised Richard most," says a woman novelist, "was the efficiency with which Eleanor handled Annabel. Her fingers seemed, of themselves to curve into the places where they would fit the spineless bundle and give it support." Places indeed! Except that right side up is best, there is not much to learn about holding a baby. There are 152 distinctly different ways—and all are right! At least all will do. A baby is so soft that anybody with a firm grip can make places for an effective hold wherever he chooses. But, "If Richard tried to take up the bundle, his fingers fell away and the bundle collapsed. And Eleanor would smile gently and send him on some masculine errand, while she soothed Annabel's feelings." You may depend upon it that Richard also smiled as soon as he was safely embarked upon some such masculine errand as playing 18 holes of golf.

HEYWOOD BROUN

One afternoon, Robert P. Tristram Coffin, the future "poet laureate" of Maine, and his father had been laboriously hoeing for several hours. Rob paused and said to his father, "I heard the flounder were biting good, down the bay."

"That's fine," his father replied. "You just keep right on hoeing, and they won't hurt you none with their biting!"

RAYMOND CHARLES SWAIN

*A dad who learned the hard way, Frank Gilbreth,
Jr., gives some advice to prospective fathers in his
book "How To Be A Father." Here he discusses his
techniques for handling baby's night time
disturbances.*

Marriage is the biggest change in a man's life, but
the next biggest change is when he and his wife
bring home their first baby. Most men recognize
both changes as for the better, although at first there
may be some gloomy moments when the bride
appears in the light of a roommate for a semester
that will never end; and the new baby appears in the
light of a house guest who will never go away.

Naturally, the new father's living habits and status
around the house will change when the baby is
brought home. Almost everything that the father
does—how loud he plays television, how much hot
water he uses, what time he wakes up in the
morning, when he eats his meals—is governed by the
demands of the baby. And the house can never be
left unmanned for a single moment, unless the baby
is removed from it as well.

Most men have been told since childhood that if
they don't get enough sleep they will ruin their
health, their nerves, their looks and their ability to
think clearly and act decisively.

A "good night's sleep" has become practically
synonymous with clean and wholesome living, and
is considered an inalienable right of all citizens in
the land of the free.

Up to the arrival of his first baby, the average

male has never experienced a recurring night-time disturbance that he could neither remedy nor move his residence away from. In the past, when any noise had disturbed his slumber, he had shouted a complaint, rapped on the ceiling, telephoned the police, turned the noise off, put it outside, thrown shoes at it, or taken some other sort of satisfying concrete action. Indeed, he had considered such action not only his personal right but his civic duty.

And now, for the first time, he finds in the baby's crying a frustrating kind of disturbance that he can't sleep through, can't move away from, and can't stop by complaints, threats, or throwing shoes. He knows very well that violence of any sort or raucous protests would intensify rather than alleviate the disturbance. And he learns quickly that the disturbance can best be terminated by the exact opposite of violence, which is gentleness.

So, after a lifetime of sound sleep, the father must not only grow accustomed to broken sleep but must discipline himself to greet the unwelcome awakenings with whispered sweet talk and lullabies, rather than coarse shouts and curses.

What has him terrified, basically, is the baby's head. He simply can't cope with it. Take away the baby's head, he reassures himself in a mental fight talk designed to bolster his courage, and infant care is duck soup.

The husband is not naïve enough to think that his dread of the baby's head is in any way unique. Indeed, he realizes that such a dread is generally attributed to new fathers. And it is precisely because he wishes to avoid the reputation of being a typical, laughable, clumsy, craven male parent that he goes to some length to conceal his fear.

This can best be accomplished by being somewhere else when it is time to pick up the baby. Such absences take careful timing and a slavish willingness to anticipate and volunteer for all sorts of disagreeable jobs. But many a father feels so strongly about his baby's head that he thinks the contrived absences are well worth the effort.

For instance, say that the baby starts crying for no particular reason at 4 A.M. If the husband lolls around in bed waiting for his wife to become wide awake, she may very well groan that she is exhausted and ask him if he would mind picking up the baby. Then the fat would be on the fire! He'd either have to tell her that, yes, being a ridiculous coward, he would mind very much indeed; or he'd have to go into the nursery, grit his teeth, and cope with the nightmare of that loose head.

What he should do, of course, is leap from bed at the very first peep out of the child, and dash into the basement. Once there, he should noisily busy himself with the furnace for the next ten or fifteen minutes, even if it be an oil burner. When he is certain that his wife has awakened and has picked up the baby, he can return and announce that the thermostat didn't seem to be working just right and that he was afraid the house was a little too cold for the infant.

The same technique works quite well during the daytime, although admittedly this keeps the husband on the jump. He may, for instance, be reading the evening paper and enjoying a cold glass of cherry smash or something before supper, when the baby starts to whimper. For the father to put down his glass and his paper and get out in the back yard to take the diapers off the line—by the time his wife calls to suggest that since she's busy getting supper he should pick up the baby—requires speed and agility. But with practice it can be done.

MINIATURE
My day-old son is plenty scrawny,
His mouth is wide with screams, or yawny,
His ears seem larger than he's needing,
His nose is flat, his chin's receding,
His skin is very, very red,
He has no hair upon his head,
And yet I'm proud as proud can be,
To hear you say he looks like me.

RICHARD ARMOUR

## A THEOLOGY FOR DAD'S DAY
Charlie Shedd quotes a famous psychiatrist as saying that "no little child will think more of God than he thinks of his father."

Shedd, a Presbyterian clergyman noted for down-to-earth writings on family matters, cites the theory in his book, *Smart Dads I Know*. He thinks the psychiatrist is right. Many will disagree with good reason: the theory presumes that God has not placed within human beings a respect for himself. Nonetheless, the comparison has some value, and Shedd suggests a good little model speech for dad to give to the kids:

"Listen to me troops. Where I'm the kind of father I should be, that's what God is like! Where I am not so hot, I hope you'll learn the all-important process of contrast. Wherever the Bible says that God is like a father, you can understand it means that God is like a perfect father. You know I'm not perfect. But I'm going to keep on trying. And I want you to know that I know I've got a long way to go."

THROUGH MANY OF THE CANDID LETTERS
PRESENTED HERE, WE CAN PEEK INTO THE
INTIMATE LIVES OF FAMOUS AND LITERATE
FATHERS. WITH LOVE AND UNDERSTANDING,
THESE FATHERS HAVE REVEALED THEMSELVES
AS WARM, COMPASSIONATE HUMAN BEINGS
ANY CHILD WOULD BE PROUD OF:

*Because Philip Mountbatten was the first eligible young man the Princess had met, and because she had fallen in love with him when she was very young, King George had the average father's misgivings about her lack of contact with other young men. In 1944, the King had written his mother that "Philip had better not think any more about (marrying Elizabeth) for the present." He continued to withhold his consent for three years, but in 1947, after Elizabeth had been taken on a tour of South Africa by her parents, there no longer was doubt about the mutual affection of the two young people. The betrothal was announced in July, and Elizabeth and Philip were married on November 20, 1947. Not long afterward, while she was on her honeymoon, the royal bride received this touching expression of her father's feelings.*

. . . I was so proud of you & thrilled at having you so close to me on our long walk in Westminster Abbey, but when I handed your hand to the Archbishop I felt I had lost something very precious. You were so calm & composed during the Service & said your words with such conviction, that I knew everything was all right.

I am so glad you wrote & told Mummy that you
think the long wait before your engagement and the
long time before the wedding was for the best. I was
rather afraid that you had thought I was being
hardhearted about it. I was so anxious for you to
come to South Africa as you know. Our family, us
four, the 'Royal Family' must remain together with
additions of course at suitable moments!! I have
watched you grow up all these years with pride
under the skillful direction of Mummy, who as you
know is the most marvellous person in the World in
my eyes, & I can, I know, always count on you, &
now Philip, to help us in our work. Your leaving us
has left a great blank in our lives but do remember
that your old home is still yours & do come back to
it as much & as often as possible. I can see that you
are sublimely happy with Philip which is right but
don't forget us is the wish of

> Your ever loving & devoted
> Papa

*Throughout his life Ring Lardner corresponded in verse—always playfully, but always, too, managing to say what he wanted to say, whether it was chiding or hopeful. His oldest son, John, was nineteen and studying in Paris after a year at Harvard when the ailing Lardner, unable to sleep, left his bed to write a letter full of fondness and good spirits.*

In New York
3 A.M. Sunday, Feb. 15, 1931
8 A.M. the same day in Paris

> The Vanderbilt Hotel
> Park Avenue at Thirty-fourth
> Street
> New York

Dear John——
Keep a hold of this letter
For fear you won't get anything better.
It is written in the "wee small" hours of the
    morning
Without an instant's warning;
I just suddenly took a notion,
Having sworn off the nightly self-administration
    of a sleeping potion,

To get out of bed and use my Underwood portable
Rather than go out and walk the streets and perhaps
    court a belle.
We are back from the South and stopping at the
    Hotel V-nde-b—t,
A place that some goose or gander built.

The food here would annoy you and pain you
More than that procurable in Pennsylvania,
And my opinion, which is seldom wrong,
Is that we won't be stopping here long.
If you should care to write us, through a sense of
    duty or pity,
Address us in care of the Bell Syndicate, 63 Park
    Row, N.Y. City.

I thought you very deftly and wittily
Described your visit to s—y Italy.
This spring, if you have another holiday,
I wish you would spend it in Montpellier
Where my mother's niece Amy Serre
Lives unless she has moved from there.
She is a widow about seventy and has a daughter
Who grew old before a suitor caughter.
But they are nice and the daughter is a musician
Who prefers playing the pianoforte to going fishing.
I shall find out whether they're still there, yes
    or no;
Meanwhile, you inform me whether you'd like to go.
And now when you think it isn't too much bother
You might write a letter to sincerely your father.

*Soon after the death of his wife, William Sydney Porter ("O. Henry") was sentenced to five years in prison on a charge of embezzlement, an affair that has never been cleared up. His eight-year-old daughter, Margaret, went to live with her maternal grandmother, who collaborated with O. Henry in obscuring the fact of his imprisonment. Below is the first letter he wrote to his little girl from the Ohio State Penitentiary.*

Hello, Margaret:

Don't you remember me? I'm a Brownie, and my name is Aldibirontiphostiphornikophokos. If you see a star shoot and say my name seventeen times before it goes out, you will find a diamond ring in the track of the first blue cow's foot you see go down the road in a snowstorm while the red roses are blooming on the tomato vines. Try it some time. I know all about Anna and Arthur Dudley, but they don't see me. I was riding by on a squirrel the other day and saw you and Arthur Dudley give some fruit to some trainmen. Anna wouldn't come out. Well good-bye, I've got to take a ride on a grasshopper. I'll just sign my first letter—"A."

*Margaret Porter was grown up before O. Henry told her the facts of his imprisonment, but he sent letters regularly during the three and a half years he spent as an Ohio convict. "Here it is summertime," he wrote shortly before his release, "and we haven't been fishing yet. Well, there's only one more month till July, and then we'll go, and no mistake."*

*In the winter of 1926-27 Sherwood Anderson had
been in Paris with his daughter Marion and his son
John, a young painter. John was still in Paris, and
Sherwood Anderson was back at his home in
Virginia, when the letter below was written:*
                    (Troutdale, Virginia, ? April, 1927)
Something I should have said in my letter yesterday.

In relation to painting.

Don't be carried off your feet by anything because
it is modern, the latest thing.

Go to the Louvre often and spend a good deal of
time before the Rembrandts, the Delacroix's.

Learn to draw. Try to make your hand so
unconsciously adept that it will put down what you
feel without your having to think of your hands.

Then you can think of the thing before you.

Draw things that have some meaning to you. An
apple, what does it mean?

The object drawn doesn't matter so much. It's
what you feel about it, what it means to you.

A masterpiece could be made of a dish of turnips.

Draw, draw, hundreds of drawing(s)

Try to remain humble. Smartness kills everything.

The object of art is not to make salable pictures. It
is to save yourself.

*The invasion of Sicily during World War II was only a few days old when Dwight D. Eisenhower paused to write a birthday letter to his son. Eisenhower at this time, according to John Gunther, "was working in a damp cubicle not bigger than ten feet by fourteen; there was a single table covered by a gray blanket and a white blotter; an oil heater was burning, but the clay floor was wet and cold. The General tossed away one of his cigarettes and asked, 'You fellows got a dry cigarette?' None of us had." In this setting, Ike wrote as follows, dated July 12, 1943:*

Dear Johnnie: This is written from my advanced CP during the early days of the Sicilian attack. The papers keep you fairly well informed of our operations, so you know that this whole force is hard at it again.

Strangely enough, for me personally, the beginning of one of these major pushes is a period of comparative inactivity, because there is so much waiting for reports, while I'm removed from my main headquarters where there is always something to keep one hustling.

The main purpose of this note is to wish you well on your birthday. You will be twenty-one—a voter if you were a civilian! I wish I could be there to shake you by the hand and say "Good luck!" As it is, this note will have to do, although possibly I'll get to send you a teletype, too.

You will note that the ink seems to sink into this paper. That is because of the dampness in this tunnel where my office is located. The weather outside is hot and dry. You may be sure I spend as little time as possible in this hole—but occasionally I have to have conferences, etc. here. . . .

It's time to go see the Admiral. He's one of my best friends—and a great fighting man. Good luck, and again, congratulations.

Devotedly,
Dad

The night you were born, I ceased being my father's boy and became my son's father. That night I began a new life.

HENRY GREGOR FELSEN

# IT'S BEAUTIFUL
*Confessions of a Confirmed Father*

One evening last fall, at a time when my son Lee was just turning three, some storm clouds gathered out over the Pacific while I was reading him a bedtime story. Clouds of any kind are a rarity in arid southern California, and when thunder started booming across the sky Lee was both curious and frightened. He interrupted the story and asked, "What's that, Daddy?"

I gave some fumbling answer about the clouds' making the noise and we went back to the book. Later the thought struck me: How many children, over how many centuries, have asked their fathers to explain thunder? (And how many fathers have known the answer?) Being asked about thunder was like entering some ancient tradition, joining a fellowship of fatherhood that must have started with Cain's first inquiries of his puzzled parents.

I like the idea of joining such a tradition. I like being the father of Lee, and of Rebecca, 23 months younger than her brother. It is one of the most interesting, enjoyable and maddening things a man can be. . . .

It's a little scary to realize how closely kids mimic their parents. Lee's favorite outfit is blue jeans "just like Daddy's." He lugs around a discarded typewriter and briefcase and declares he is "going to work." One day at the park I noticed him as he held a basketball and gazed up at the basket towering ten feet in the air. I watched as time and again, like a pint-sized Sisyphus, he propelled the ball about a foot into the air. Then he started all over. . . .

Actually my kids teach me as much as I teach them—maybe more. For one thing, they help me understand my own parents a lot better, in all their frailty and folly. If you can't really understand combat until you've been under fire, you probably can't understand parenthood either unless you have tried it. . . .

When I come home at night and the two of them burst through the door, running down the walk to greet me, the world is a beautiful place. No matter what else has happened, it's beautiful.

STEVEN V. ROBERTS

# THE WAY TO KNOW A FATHER

No man knows his father till he sees
His father in the son upon his knees;
The best way for a man to understand
His father is to hold him by the hand.

When he is small enough, a father's face
Is full of starriness and looks like space
Above the trees upon an August night,
And his dark future is unfathomed light.

What his son and his son's sons will be
Is there for any man to see;
The father sits with wonder in his gaze
To see the sure design of his own days.

What was behind the sorrow and the lust,
What was behind his father's work in dust
Was holy, single life unearthly keen,
Clean as the petals on a star are clean.

A grandson tells what no man dares to tell
When he is deep in living and feels well:
That any son is more than one man's heir
And wears all proud men's glory on his hair.

ROBERT P. TRISTRAM COFFIN

# Acknowledgments

The editor and the publisher have made every effort to trace the ownership of all copyrighted material and to secure permission from copyright holders of such material. In the event of any question arising as to the use of any material the publisher and editor, while expressing regret for inadvertent error, will be pleased to make the necessary corrections in future printings. Thanks are due to the following authors, publishers, publications and agents for permission to use the material indicated.

RICHARD ARMOUR, for "Miniature."

PATRICIA M. BROUN, for "Holding the Baby," by Heywood Broun, from *The Collected Edition of Heywood Broun.*

ROBERT P. T. COFFIN, JR., for "The Way to Know a Father," by Robert P. Tristram Coffin.

THOMAS Y. CROWELL COMPANY, INC., for excerpt from *How to Be a Father* by Frank Gilbreth, Jr. copyright © 1958 by Frank Gilbreth, Jr.

CURTIS BROWN, LTD., for "Daddy Won't Listen to Reason" by Robert Thomas Allen, reprinted by permission of Curtis Brown, Ltd., and Robert Thomas Allen.

THE DIAL PRESS, for excerpts from "My Father" from *Daybreak* by Joan Baez, copyright © 1966, 1968 by Joan Baez.

DOUBLEDAY & COMPANY, INC., for excerpt from *Who Am I, God,* by Marjorie Holmes, copyright © 1970 by Marjorie Holmes Mighell.

HER MAJESTY QUEEN ELIZABETH II, for "A Letter to Princess Elizabeth" by her father, His Majesty King George VI, reprinted by the gracious permission of Her Majesty.

AILEEN FISHER, for "A Wonderful Man" from *That's Why,* published by Thomas Nelson & Sons, 1946.

HARCOURT BRACE JOVANOVICH, INC., for excerpt from *The People, Yes,* by Carl Sandburg, copyright 1936, by Harcourt Brace Jovanovich, Inc., renewed 1964 by Carl Sandburg.

HARPER & ROW, PUBLISHERS, INC., for excerpt from *Eisenhower, the Man and the Symbol,* by John Gunther, copyright 1951, 1952 by Harper & Row, Publishers, Inc., for excerpt from *A Joyful Noise* by Janet Gillespie, copyright © 1971 by Janet Gillespie.

ESTATE OF RALF KIRCHER, for excerpt from "Your Best Friend is Your Father" from *There's a Fly in this Room,* copyright 1946 by Ralf Kircher.

ALFRED A. KNOPF, INC., for excerpt from *How It Was* by Mary Welsh Hemingway, copyright 1951, © 1956, 1963, 1965, 1976, by Mary Welsh Hemingway.

LITTLE, BROWN AND COMPANY, for letter of Sherwood Anderson to his son, John, from *Letters of Sherwood Anderson,* selected and edited with an Introduction and Notes by Howard Mumford Jones in association with Walter B. Rideout, copyright 1953 by Eleanor Anderson.

REDBOOK, for excerpt from "Confessions of a Confirmed Father" by Steven V. Roberts, reprinted from Redbook Magazine, June, 1973, copyright © 1973 by The Redbook Publishing Company; for excerpt from "Reflections of a Father Who

Set in Continental roman and
italic, a phototype version
of Trump Medieval.
Designed by Thomas James Aaron